AMISH QUILTING PATTERNS

56 Full-Size Ready-to-Use Designs
and Complete Instructions

GWEN MARSTON &
JOE CUNNINGHAM

DOVER PUBLICATIONS, INC.
New York

Published in Canada by General Publishing Company, Ltd.,
30 Lesmill Road, Don Mills, Toronto, Ontario.
Published in the United Kingdom by Constable and Company, Ltd.,
10 Orange Street, London WC2H 7EG.

*Amish Quilting Patterns: 56 Full-Size Ready-to-Use Designs
and Complete Instructions* is a new work, first published
by Dover Publications, Inc., in 1987.

International Standard Book Number: 0-486-25326-0

Manufactured in the United States of America
Dover Publications, Inc., 31 East 2nd Street, Mineola, N.Y. 11501

Introduction

When quilting was invented thousands of years ago, it filled a simple need—warmth. Two or three layers of fabric sewn together were warmer and sturdier than one. Quilting retained this original function but, with the rise of the American patchwork quilt, it came to have a decorative function as well.

On some quilts, the quilting is nearly invisible, its subtle outlines and cross-hatchings playing a secondary role to the patchwork, while on all-white quilts the quilting carries the entire design. On still other quilts, the quilting works in partnership with the piecing, with each given equal attention.

A good example of this last approach to quilting is the work found on pre-1940 Old Order Amish quilts. Large, simple geometric designs are covered with handsome, elaborate, organic shapes in quilting. At a distance these quilts resemble hard-edged abstract paintings. Up close, the quilting seems to lead a life of its own, separate from the color design. The development of this highly individual quilting aesthetic probably would not have been possible outside the cloistered Amish community, where it would have clashed with mainstream quilting. Indeed, as

Amish farmers moved to the Midwest and new communities, Amish quilts came more and more to resemble quilts from the "outside." In fact, Amish quilts today are no different in appearance than quilts made anywhere. No particular event marked a change in Amish quilts, but if their history is seen as a progression from purely Amish design to purely mainstream design, then 1940 marks the point where mainstream elements begin to outweigh traditional ones.

Lancaster County Amish Quilts

In the earliest Amish settlements in Lancaster County, Pennsylvania, quilting was at its height between 1850 and 1925. The classic pieced patterns from this period are simplified medallion types—that is, each quilt is made of one large design, rather than a number of small, repeated designs (*Diagram 1*). The patterns were few, usually variations of the Center Diamond, Sunshine and Shadow or Bars. These were more *formats* than patterns, allowing wide leeway in personal interpretation of color, propor-

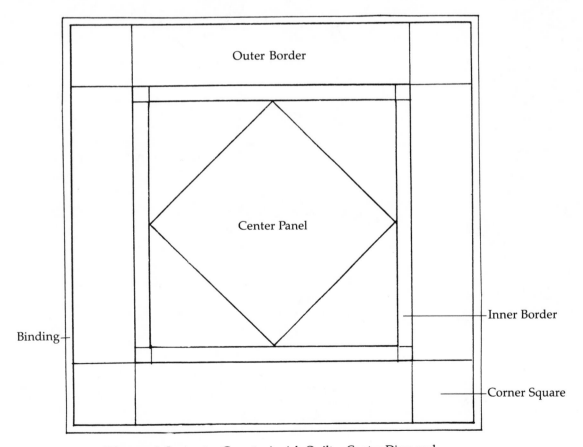

Diagram 1. Lancaster County Amish Quilt—Center Diamond.

3

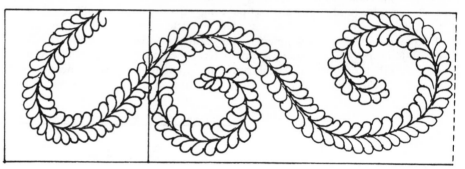

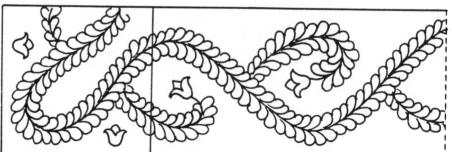

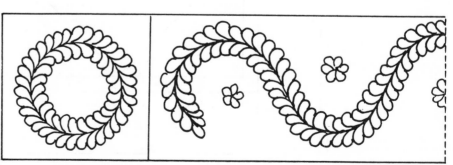

Diagram 2. Six different feather borders.

tion and scale. Quilting was similar, with a few patterns, widely interpreted.

The outer borders of these quilts were usually twelve to fourteen inches wide, allowing for large-scale quilting motifs such as baskets (*Plates 2* and *3*), fiddlehead ferns (*Plates 4,5* and *6*) and feathers.

Lancaster County Amish quilts often featured graceful, elaborate feather designs. Only rarely did a quilter choose to fill in the background with diagonal lines or cross-hatching; more often, small, self-contained motifs such as hearts, tulips, pumpkin seeds or stars were used.

No two of these feather designs are exactly alike, but there are common variations on the theme represented by the patterns shown in *Diagram 2*. The corner resolution and one half of each design is shown. Such designs can easily be drafted to fit any size border as follows: Cut a piece of paper the size of one half of the border and divide the paper into units of equal length. Sketch in the spine of the feather and refine this line; then draw in the feathers. Transfer the design to the quilt top (see "How to Use the Patterns," page 7). With a little practice, it is possible to draft the spine on paper, transfer it to the quilt and draw the feathers freehand directly on the fabric.

Individual plumes (*Plate 1*) were another interesting border design. Standing on their ends, they were sometimes arranged to face the midpoint of the border, sometimes to march in one direction around the quilt.

The narrower inner borders of Lancaster County quilts were usually quilted with a pumpkin-seed variation (*Plate 7*, lower left and *Plate 13*). Although not as common as the pumpkin seed, grape and grape-leaf designs were sometimes used (*Plates 8* and *9*); these designs were also used on the long panels of Bars quilts. Very occasionally, a cable was used (*Plate 18*, right), although these designs are much more commonly found on Midwestern Amish quilts.

In some quilts—Sunshine and Shadow and Bars for instance—the entire center panel was quilted with cross-hatching. However, the Center Diamonds, Sawtooth Center Diamonds and Center Squares have designs in the center panel that rank with the finest done anywhere in the history of quiltmaking. Generally, these designs consist of feathers, stars (*Plate 11*) and bouquets (*Plate 14*). Smaller motifs were often used to fill in the open spaces left around these larger motifs.

Most Lancaster County Amish quilts fall into a single category, defined by these general guidelines:

Square, medallion format

Wide outside border, quilted with large designs, usually feathers, baskets or fiddlehead ferns

Narrow inner border, usually quilted with a pumpkin-seed design

A center field filled either with cross-hatching or feathers, stars and floral sprays

Black thread used for quilting

One- to two-inch-wide bindings cut on the straight, usually applied by machine

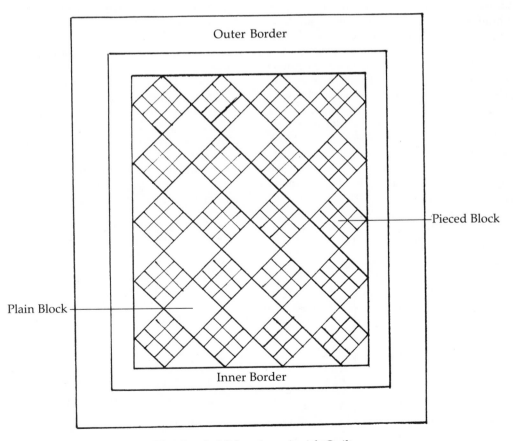

Diagram 3. Midwestern Amish Quilt.

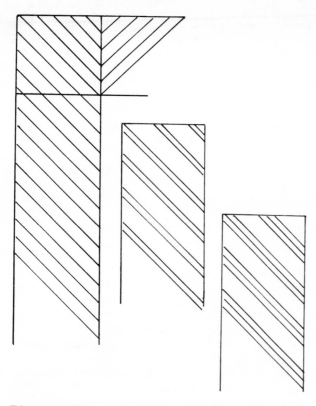

Diagram 4. Diagonal quilting patterns for outer borders.

Midwestern Amish Quilts

As farmland grew scarce in eastern Pennsylvania, new Amish communities sprang up in Ohio, Michigan, Indiana, Illinois, Iowa and Kansas. It must have been during and soon after the move to these new farm towns that many Amish quiltmakers saw their first non-Amish quilts. These new quilts must have seemed exotic and full of ideas to explore, for Midwestern Amish quilts soon resembled the quilts of the "English" or non-Amish as much as they did the quilts of their Old Order ancestors. The most striking change was the newly adapted block style of construction. Some Pennsylvania Amish quilts had been made of blocks, but they were rare. Around 1900 these new Midwestern quilts began to use blocks almost exclusively (*Diagram 3*).

Other changes happened quickly—the square format was abandoned for the rectangular; black and a wider range of colors were used more often; outer borders became narrower. While the piecing grew more complex and varied, the quilting became simpler.

As the outer borders became narrower, the quilting designs used on them changed. Cables (*Plates 15, 16, 17, 19, 30* and *31*) and diagonal lines (*Diagram 4*) were the most common motifs, but tulips (*Plates 20, 21* and *29*), fans (*Plate 23*) and clamshells (*Plate 40*) were frequently used. Feathers became much less common; when they were used, they were much simpler than those used on Lancaster County quilts (*Plate 22*).

Nearly all of the inner borders of Midwestern Amish quilts have quilting designs composed of two elements—a pointed oval known variously as the "orange peel" or "pumpkin seed" and the tulip (*Plates 18, 19, 21, 24, 25, 26, 27* and *29*). *Plate 41* shows an example of one of the few inner borders not composed of one or both of these elements.

The blocks of the Midwestern quilts were almost always set together diagonally with plain blocks between them. The pieced blocks were usually quilted with single, double or even triple diagonal lines across the surface of the block. Cross-hatching was the next most common method of quilting these blocks, and outline quilting was also used.

There are almost as many quilting designs for the plain blocks as there are quilts, but most are personal interpretations of the tulip (*Plates 34, 35* and *42*), the lyre (*Plates 36, 37* and *41*) or the feather wreath (*Plates 30, 31, 32* and *33*). Diagonal lines were also used to fill these plain blocks (*Diagram 5*).

These, then are the major characteristics of Midwestern Amish quilts:

Rectangular, block style format, often with black or a broader range of colors

Narrower outside border, often quilted with cables, diagonals or fans

Inner border, usually quilted with an "orange peel" variation

Straight lines quilted through pieced blocks

Wide use of tulips, few feathers

Black thread used for quilting

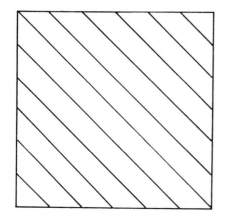

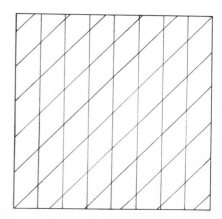

Diagram 5. Diagonal quilting patterns for plain blocks.

General Instructions for Quilting

How to Use the Patterns

The 56 full-size quilting patterns shown on Plates 1–42 can be used to create your own Amish-style quilt. Designs for outer and inner borders are given, as well as designs for center panels and plain blocks.

The easiest way to transfer these designs to fabric is simply to trace them onto your fabric with a Berol Verithin pencil (white for dark fabric, silver for light). With dark or printed fabric, make a light table by placing a lamp below a piece of glass. If necessary, diffuse the light by taping more layers of paper to the glass.

There are several other methods for preparing the patterns and transferring them to your fabric. Four of these methods are described here.

Making a Perforated Pattern

For this method you will need scissors, a sewing machine, fine sandpaper, French chalk or cornstarch (for dark fabrics), cocoa, cinnamon or snuff (for light fabrics) and a silver or white Berol Verithin artist's pencil or a No. 3 pencil.

Cut out the desired pattern, leaving at least ¼" to ½" of blank paper all around. Remove the pressure foot from your sewing machine and place the pattern directly beneath the needle. Set your stitch length for 6-stitches-per-inch. Begin "sewing" very slowly by turning the wheel to raise and lower the needle while carefully guiding the pattern so the needle pierces the paper along the design lines (*Diagram 6*). Continue until your entire design has been pierced in this manner. The patterns can also be perforated by using a pushpin, tiny nail or another sharp instrument; keep the perforations even and centered exactly over the lines.

Remove the paper from the sewing machine and gently sand the wrong side to open up the holes completely and remove excess paper that may be protruding from the

Diagram 7. Rubbing powder through the holes of a perforated pattern to transfer the design.

wrong side. Then, pin the pattern to your fabric and rub powder through the holes with a cotton ball or soft cloth (*Diagram 7*). Carefully remove the pattern from the fabric without disturbing the powder. Go over all of the powdered design lines with your pencil to make them permanent enough to last through the quilting process. Then, shake or brush away the powder.

Making a Quilting Stencil

For this method you will need scissors, illustration board or heavy cardboard, rubber cement, an X-ACTO knife, fine sandpaper and a silver or white Berol Verithin artist's pencil or a No. 3 pencil.

Cut out the desired pattern, leaving at least ¼" of blank paper all around. Using rubber cement, glue the pattern onto illustration board or cardboard. Allow the glue to dry, then, using an X-ACTO knife, carefully cut out the pattern along the lines of the design.

For simple quilting patterns with interior spaces, either cut out the spaces using an X-ACTO knife or cut channels in the template along the lines that must be transferred (*Diagram 8*); "ladders" must be left in the channels to allow

Diagram 6. Making a perforated pattern.

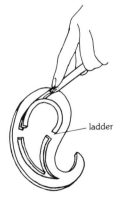
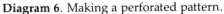

ladder

Diagram 8. Cutting channels in a quilting stencil.

interior spaces to remain attached to the template. The channels must be wide enough to accommodate your sharpened pencil point. For complicated interior lines, cut channels for the major lines, then draw the remainder of the pattern freehand after the outline of the template has been drawn on the fabric.

After all outlines, spaces and channels have been cut, carefully sand all rough edges of the stencil with fine sandpaper, making the illustration board or cardboard align perfectly with the lines on the quilting pattern.

Position the quilting stencil on your fabric and trace lightly along the edges with a well-sharpened pencil. After the outline has been transferred, trace along each channel or interior space to transfer inner design lines. Draw in any extra design lines after the pattern has been removed.

A quilting stencil can also be made from clear plastic or Mylar, which may be found in art-supply stores or quilt shops.

To make a plastic stencil, position the plastic over the pattern and trace all the design lines using a marking pen or a ballpoint pen or stylus that will leave an impression on the plastic. Carefully cut channels for the design lines using an X-ACTO knife.

Two Other Methods for Using the Patterns

The quilting designs can be traced onto tracing paper or Mylar and transferred to your fabric using a tracing wheel and dressmaker's carbon paper. After tracing the design, pin the Mylar or tracing paper to your fabric, leaving two edges free. Slip dressmaker's carbon paper (white or yellow for dark fabrics; red, blue or yellow for light fabrics) face down between the pattern and the fabric. Do not pin the carbon because the pins will leave marks. Carefully go over all of the lines with a tracing wheel (*Diagram 9*); use a wheel with "teeth" that will leave a dotted line.

Another method can be used. It is called "needle-marking" and is used primarily by quilters who do not mark the entire quilt top at one time, but who mark individual designs as they go along. This marking is done after the quilt top, batting and backing have been assembled and the quilt is already in the frame.

Cut out the desired pattern and carefully trim away excess paper close to the edge of the design. Position the

Diagram 9. Using a tracing wheel and dressmaker's carbon to transfer a quilting design.

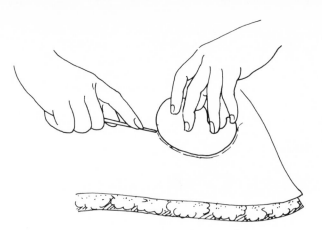

Diagram 10. Needle-marking a quilting design.

pattern on the quilt top and trace around the edge with a blunt needle such as a large thick yarn needle, leaving a crease mark on the fabric. This method is also called "scratching" but the material should not actually be scratched; the needle should be held at a sharp angle and pressed firmly into the fabric (*Diagram 10*). One can then quilt along the clearly defined indentations made with the needle.

Quilting Equipment

Needles

Quilting needles can be purchased in sizes 7–10; these needles are also called "betweens." The higher the number, the smaller the needle. The tightness of the weave, the size of your hand and the thickness of the batting will dictate the best needle size for you. The average needle is size 8.

Basting Thread

Any strong thread that will hold up to the stress of the frame or hoop is acceptable. Try to use a light-colored thread that will contrast with your fabric and quilting thread; this will make it easier to find and remove your basting thread after you have finished quilting. Do not use dark thread which may leave shadows after the basting is removed.

Quilting Thread

100% cotton quilting thread should be used. There are several brands and a wide range of colors from which to choose. It is treated to prevent knotting and to ensure that it slides smoothly through the quilt layers as you work. If you use regular cotton thread instead of quilting thread, you should run each length of thread across a piece of beeswax or paraffin before you quilt it. Traditionally, most Amish quilting was done with black thread, but colored thread was also used, sometimes blending with the background fabric and sometimes contrasting with it.

Tape Measure

This will be needed when marking placements for specific quilting motifs.

Scissors

Use one pair of household scissors for cutting the paper patterns; use a pair of very sharp scissors when quilting to clip threads—small embroidery scissors work well.

Large Safety Pins

These are used to initially hold the three layers of the quilt together before basting.

Quilter's Pins

These are used to attach the quilt back to the stretchers and the batting and quilt top to the quilt back when using a frame.

Iron

The quilt top and lining must be perfectly ironed before assembly; a steam iron would best accomplish this.

Batting

Old Amish quilts are generally thinner than other quilts, so we prefer to use very thin batts when we work in this style. *Cotton outing flannel* works fine but is, of course, extremely flat. Thin *cotton* or *wool batts* are usually thicker. We use the *Fairfield Cotton Classic batt*, which is 80% cotton and 20% polyester. It is bonded to be easy to work with. Follow the manufacturer's instructions for pre-soaking and drying it before use. *Polyester batts* are easiest to needle, but they have a tendency to "beard," or work their way through the fabric, with dark, Amish colors.

Thimbles

Use a flat-faced metal thimble rather than one with a rounded end. The thimble should fit snugly on the middle finger of your right hand if you are right-handed, or the middle finger of your left hand if you are left-handed.

Quilting Frames and Hoops

The purpose of using a quilting frame or hoop is to maintain an easy, even tension on the three layers of the quilt sandwich—the backing, batting and top—keeping the layers from sagging or shifting and enabling you to quilt evenly. The selection of a quilting frame or hoop is a matter of individual choice. There are advantages and disadvantages to using either one, and some quilters prefer not using one at all. Basically the decision of what type of frame to use is based on the amount of space available and where you want to quilt. Full frames allow even tension on the quilt layers at all times, but take up a great deal of room. Hoops are more versatile, enabling you to quilt in various places if you wish, but great care must be taken initially to prevent the layers of the quilt sandwich from shifting.

Full Frame

To make your own frame, you will need four 1" × 2" pine boards and four 2" C-clamps. Cut two of the boards 12" longer than your quilt top and the other two 12" wider than your quilt top. Staple long, folded strips of sturdy fabric along the entire length of each board, with the fold projecting about ½" beyond the edge. Rest the two longer boards (the stretchers) on the backs of four chairs and place the two shorter boards (the rollers) across them. The fabric strips should be on top of each board, pointing toward the inside of the frame.

Make the quilt back about 3" longer and 3" wider than the top. Use quilting thread to whip-stitch the ends of the back, wrong side up, to the fabric strips on the rollers. Once the back is sewn to the strips, clamp one roller to the stretchers. Brace the other end of each stretcher, one at a time, against your thigh, pull the loose roller tight and clamp it. Pin the sides of the backing fabric to the fabric on the stretchers about every 2". The back should now be like a trampoline, with no wrinkles, firmly sewn to the rollers and pinned to the stretchers.

Spread the batting on the taut quilt back and smooth out all wrinkles. Center the quilt top, right side up, on the batting and smooth out all of its wrinkles. Starting in the middle of one side, pin through all three layers about ¼" in from the edge, every 2" around the quilt. Work in one direction only, pulling the top taut with the pins. Pull it tight enough to smooth it out, but not so tight that you pull the borders or blocks out of shape.

No basting is required. Quilting proceeds all around the edge of the quilt as far in as you can reach, usually about 10". Once the edge is quilted you can unclamp the rollers, unpin about 10" of the sides, roll the quilted part up like a scroll and reclamp the rollers (*Diagram 11*). Do one end at a time, and brace the stretchers against your thigh for tension. As you quilt, check the underside of the quilt occasionally to make sure there are no wrinkles. If wrinkles develop, readjust the boards and clamps for more tension.

Even if you use a hoop, the full-size frame is still the best way to get started. Use the same procedure for installing the quilt sandwich in the frame, but baste instead of quilting, rolling the quilt inward to reach the middle. When the quilt is all basted you can take it out of the frame and quilt it in the hoop, secure in the knowledge that you will have no wrinkles or puckers. Unlike quilting in the frame, however, hoop quilting starts in the middle and works outward.

Roller Frame

Like the full frame, the roller frame consists of two rollers the width of the quilt and two stretchers that hold the rollers in place to keep the quilt taut. In the roller frame, however, the stretchers are much shorter than the quilt; they are just long enough to allow the quilter to reach all

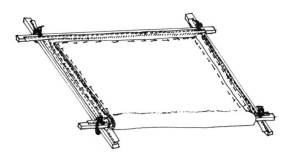

Diagram 11. Full-size frame with one end sewn and the other end already rolled.

areas of the exposed quilt. Because the frame is smaller than the quilt, the quilt sandwich should be thoroughly basted before putting it in the frame to keep the back from sagging.

To set up a quilt in a roller frame, assemble the quilt back, batting and top; see below for assembly instructions. Attach each end of the quilt to the frame by sewing all three layers to the apron on each roller; roll the ends of the quilt evenly onto each roller until the quilt is held taut between them. Pin the sides of the quilt back to the aprons on the stretchers, keeping an even tension across the quilt. The quilting can now proceed. When the exposed area has been fully quilted, remove the pins and roll the quilted portion out of the way, exposing a fresh area; reattach the pins. Continue in this manner until the quilt top is finished.

Quilting Hoop

A round wooden quilting hoop about 24″ in diameter is an excellent alternative to a full or roller frame. It is portable yet provides a working area large enough to prevent frequent repositioning. Wooden hoops should have an adjustable outer frame; this usually consists of wooden blocks through which a bolt is tightened. The quilt sandwich must be thoroughly basted if the work is to be quilted in a hoop.

Assembling the Quilt Sandwich

Once the quilt top is completed and ready for quilting, the quilt sandwich must be assembled. We feel it is best to baste your quilt in a frame no matter how you choose to quilt it. But if a frame is not available at all there is another method.

Iron the top and back to make sure there are no wrinkles. Spread the backing, wrong side up, on a large

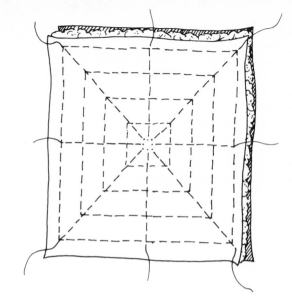

Diagram 13. Additional basting—recommended if using a quilting hoop.

flat surface (usually an uncovered floor is the best place—if possible, take up the rug to prevent pinning your quilt layers to it). Spread your batting evenly over the backing; this job is relatively easy if using polyester batting. If using cotton or wool batting, spread it *carefully* over the backing using the utmost caution to prevent holes or thin spots from forming.

Once the batting is smoothly in place, carefully lay your quilt top right side up, over the batting. Smooth and ease the quilt top so it fits squarely and evenly over the other two layers. Using large safety pins, secure the three layers starting from the center and working out toward the sides and corners; use as many pins as you feel are necessary to keep the layers from shifting. Next, thoroughly baste the three layers together following *Diagram 12*. Use a long strand of basting thread, knotted at the end. Start in the center and work outward toward the edges of the quilt diagonally, horizontally and vertically. The stitches can be quite long, but you must keep two things in mind at all times while basting. First, the basting stitches must secure all three layers of the quilt sandwich. Second, the backing must be kept completely smooth at all times; check constantly (by feel) for any pulls or wrinkles in the backing and correct them immediately. If you take your time in the basting process, you can practically be assured of superb results in the quilting process. If using a hoop, it is recommended that you baste between the other lines as shown in *Diagram 13*. This is not necessary if you are using a roller frame.

How to Quilt

While neatness and precision are essential, the most important aspect of quilting is rhythm. Rhythm will not only make quilting more relaxing and enjoyable, but it will contribute toward making your stitches neat and even. The best way to achieve this rhythm is to sit comfortably

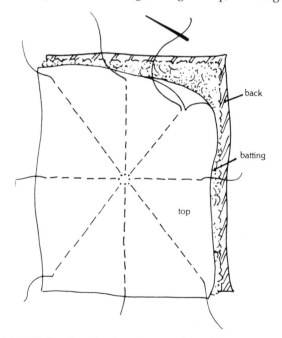

Diagram 12. Basting the three layers of the quilt sandwich together.

in front of your frame with your sewing hand on top of the quilt and the other hand below—ready to guide the needle in its up-and-down motion. Use a thimble on the middle finger of your sewing hand. Remember that every quilting stitch must go through all three layers of the quilt sandwich and the stitches (and the space between them) should have the same appearance on each side of the quilt.

Use one strand of thread in your quilting needle. Make a small knot at the end of the thread and insert the needle through the top and batting only. Tug the thread until the knot pops below the surface of the quilt top to be buried in the batting. Some quilters prefer to have several working needles going at the same time, especially when quilting a border or filling. If several needles are in use at the same time, the work can advance evenly across the quilt. This, however, is a matter of personal choice.

Quilting stitches are actually running stitches. With the threaded end of the needle resting against the thimble on

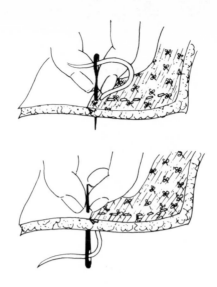

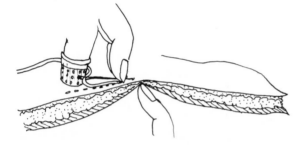

Diagram 14. The quilting stitch—guide the needle through the surface until it makes contact with the finger below the quilt.

Diagram 15. Pressing against the quilt with your thumb to "help" the needle back to the surface.

Diagram 16. Working stab stitches across a seam allowance.

the hand above the quilt, guide the needle at a slight angle into the quilt's surface so the point of the needle makes contact with the index finger on the hand below the quilt (Diagram 14). The finger below the quilt should be exerting enough pressure to cause a ridge in the surface, enabling you to determine exactly where to aim the point of the needle. As the needle touches the finger below the quilt, direct it back to the surface of the quilt top and pull needle and thread through, completing the first stitch. The needle can be "helped" back to the surface by pressing against the quilt with your thumb (Diagram 15); this will also aid in keeping the spaces between the stitches even.

When you are working on a patchwork quilt, there are times when the quilting stitches must cross seamlines. It is difficult to work the running stitch across the extra thickness made by the seam allowances, so work two to four stab stitches across the difficult area (Diagram 16), giving an extra tug to the thread with each of these stab stitches.

To end a line of quilting, slip the needle between the layers and back to the surface about 1" away. Bring it up in a seam or a quilting stitch if no seam is handy. Repeat this twice. Pull needle and thread to the surface, hold taut and clip the thread close to the quilt top.

Metric Conversion Chart

CONVERTING INCHES TO CENTIMETERS AND YARDS TO METERS

mm — millimeters   cm — centimeters   m — meters

INCHES INTO MILLIMETERS AND CENTIMETERS
(Slightly rounded off for convenience)

inches	mm		cm	inches	cm	inches	cm	inches	cm
⅛	3mm			5	12.5	21	53.5	38	96.5
¼	6mm			5½	14	22	56	39	99
⅜	10mm	or	1cm	6	15	23	58.5	40	101.5
½	13mm	or	1.3cm	7	18	24	61	41	104
⅝	15mm	or	1.5cm	8	20.5	25	63.5	42	106.5
¾	20mm	or	2cm	9	23	26	66	43	109
⅞	22mm	or	2.2cm	10	25.5	27	68.5	44	112
1	25mm	or	2.5cm	11	28	28	71	45	114.5
1¼	32mm	or	3.2cm	12	30.5	29	73.5	46	117
1½	38mm	or	3.8cm	13	33	30	76	47	119.5
1¾	45mm	or	4.5cm	14	35.5	31	79	48	122
2	50mm	or	5cm	15	38	32	81.5	49	124.5
2½	65mm	or	6.5cm	16	40.5	33	84	50	127
3	75mm	or	7.5cm	17	43	34	86.5		
3½	90mm	or	9cm	18	46	35	89		
4	100mm	or	10cm	19	48.5	36	91.5		
4½	115mm	or	11.5cm	20	51	37	94		

YARDS TO METERS
(Slightly rounded off for convenience)

yards	meters	yards	meters	yards	meters	yards	meters	yards	meters
⅛	0.15	2⅛	1.95	4⅛	3.80	6⅛	5.60	8⅛	7.45
¼	0.25	2¼	2.10	4¼	3.90	6¼	5.75	8¼	7.55
⅜	0.35	2⅜	2.20	4⅜	4.00	6⅜	5.85	8⅜	7.70
½	0.50	2½	2.30	4½	4.15	6½	5.95	8½	7.80
⅝	0.60	2⅝	2.40	4⅝	4.25	6⅝	6.10	8⅝	7.90
¾	0.70	2¾	2.55	4¾	4.35	6¾	6.20	8¾	8.00
⅞	0.80	2⅞	2.65	4⅞	4.50	6⅞	6.30	8⅞	8.15
1	0.95	3	2.75	5	4.60	7	6.40	9	8.25
1⅛	1.05	3⅛	2.90	5⅛	4.70	7⅛	6.55	9⅛	8.35
1¼	1.15	3¼	3.00	5¼	4.80	7¼	6.65	9¼	8.50
1⅜	1.30	3⅜	3.10	5⅜	4.95	7⅜	6.75	9⅜	8.60
1½	1.40	3½	3.20	5½	5.05	7½	6.90	9½	8.70
1⅝	1.50	3⅝	3.35	5⅝	5.15	7⅝	7.00	9⅝	8.80
1¾	1.60	3¾	3.45	5¾	5.30	7¾	7.10	9¾	8.95
1⅞	1.75	3⅞	3.55	5⅞	5.40	7⅞	7.20	9⅞	9.05
2	1.85	4	3.70	6	5.50	8	7.35	10	9.15

Plate 1

Reverse pattern along center line to complete design.

Center

Plate 2

Plate 3

Tape pattern pieces together at broken line.

Plate 4

Tape pattern pieces together at broken line.

Plate 5

Plate 6

Plate 7

Plate 8

Tape pattern pieces together at broken line.

Plate 9

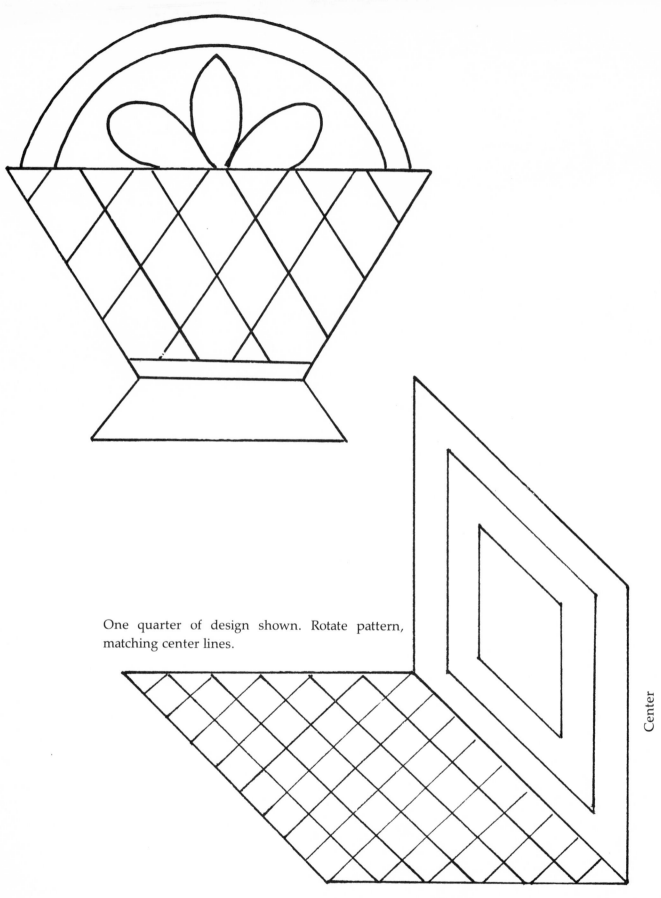

One quarter of design shown. Rotate pattern, matching center lines.

Center

Center

Plate 10

Center

Center

To complete design, rotate pattern, matching center lines.

Plate 11

Plate 12

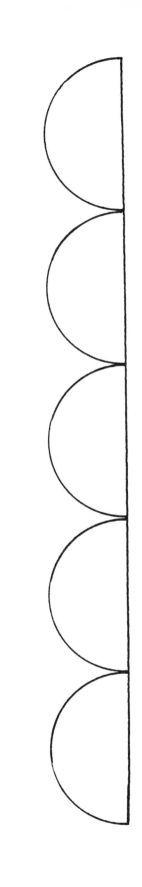

Plate 13

Tape pattern pieces together at broken line.

Plate 14

Plate 15

Tape pattern pieces together at broken line.

Plate 16

Tape pattern pieces together
at broken line.

Plate 17

Plate 18

Plate 19

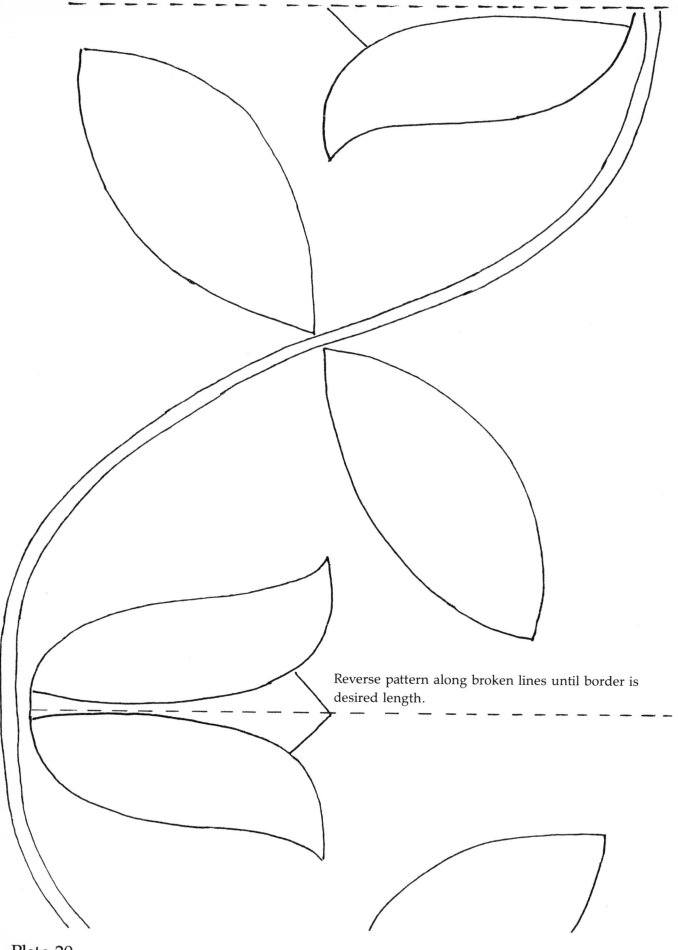

Reverse pattern along broken lines until border is desired length.

Plate 20

Reverse pattern along broken lines until border is desired length.

Plate 21

Plate 22

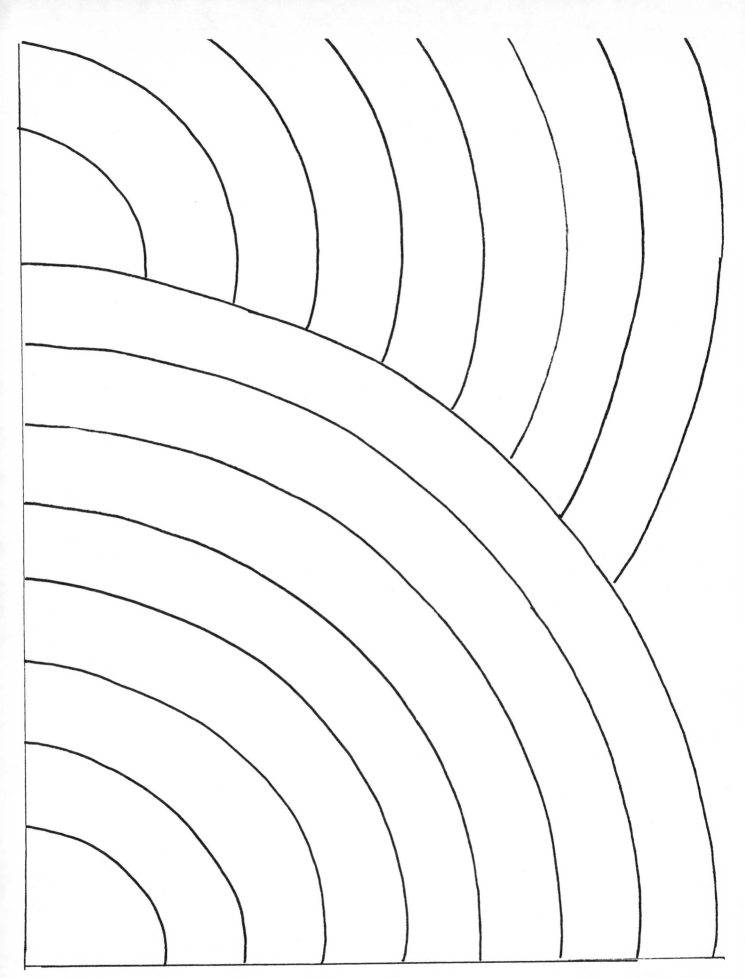

Plate 23

Tape to pattern on Plate 25 at broken line.

Plate 24

Center

Reverse pattern along center line to complete design.

Tape to pattern on Plate 24 at broken line.

Plate 25

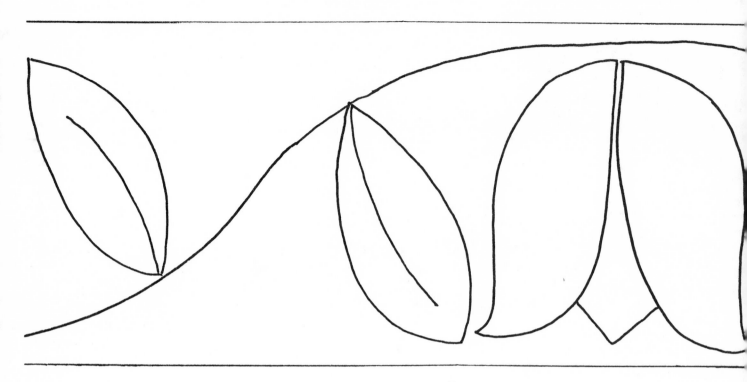

Tape pattern pieces together at broken line.

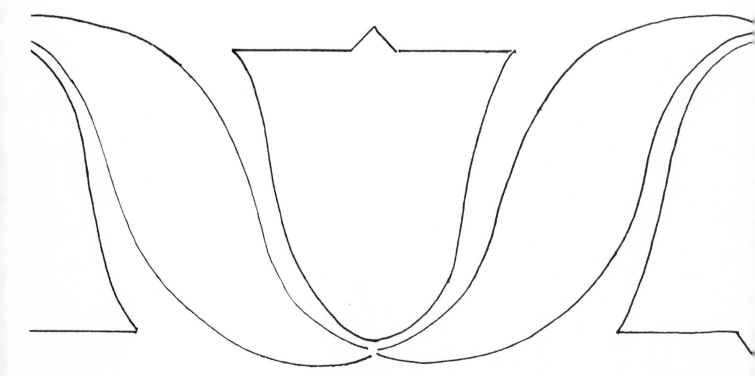

Plate 26

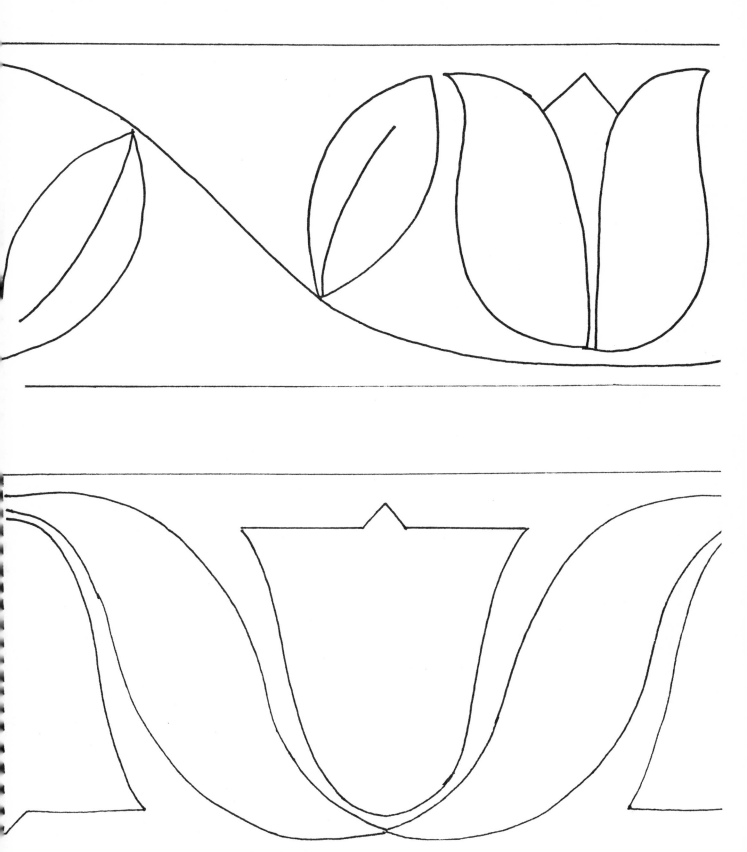

Tape pattern pieces together at broken line.

Plate 27

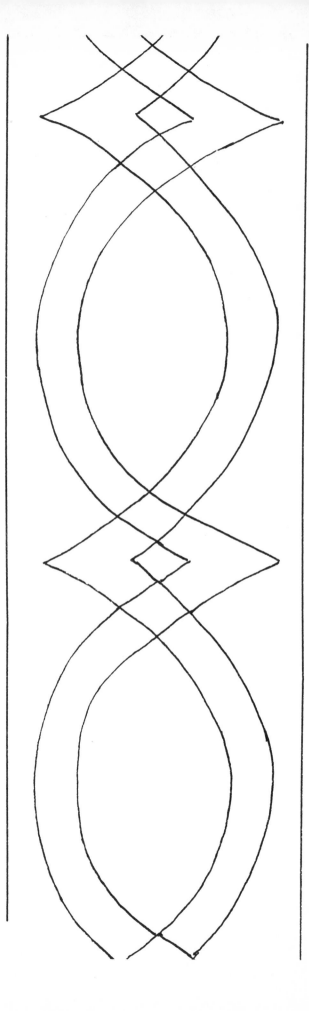

Plate 28

Reverse pattern along broken lines until border is desired length.

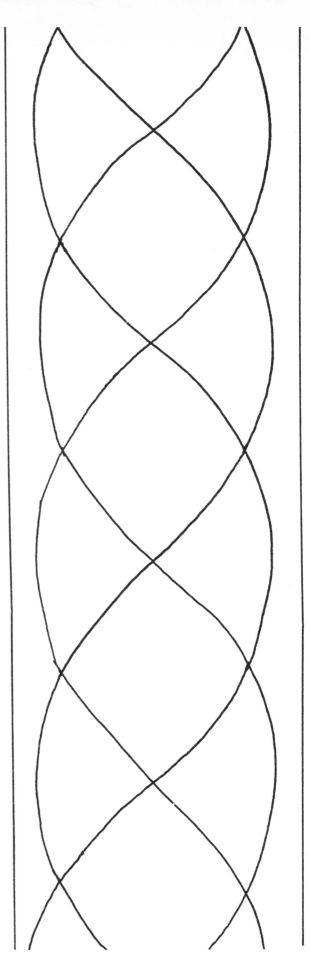

Plate 29

Tape pattern pieces together at broken line.

Plate 30

Plate 31

Plate 32

Tape pattern pieces together at broken line.

Center

Reverse pattern along center line to complete design.

Plate 33

Plate 34

Tape pattern pieces together at broken line.

Tape pattern pieces together at broken line.

Plate 35

Plate 36

Plate 37

Plate 38

Plate 39

Plate 40

Plate 41

Reverse pattern along center line to complete design.

Plate 42